SLEEPING WITH SAPPHO

SLEEPING WITH SAPPHO

STEPHEN VINCENT

BLAZEVOX[BOOKS]
Buffalo, New York

First Edition
ISBN: 978-1-60964-443-7
Library of Congress Control Number: 2023940301

BlazeVOX [books]
131 Euclid Ave
Kenmore, NY 14217
Editor@blazevox.org

publisher of weird little books

BlazeVOX [books]

blazevox.org

21 20 19 18 17 16 15 14 13 12 01 02 03 04 05 06 07 08 09 10 11

BlazeVOX

Acknowledgments

With gratitude for previous publication of some of these poems and fragments in magazines that include *New American Writing*, *Fascicles*, *On Edit*, *Shampoo*, and *26*.

SLEEPING WITH SAPPHO

1.

Gone from her: jagged alabaster underfoot

No ripe peach orchard

No cedar glow, no candle lit

No amber flame

Boiled saltwater percolates steam into

Wilted roses into rank deadheads:

What was radiant glimmers nowhere

No sleep will warm her breasts

The goat's kids chomp the grass bare

Sacrifice without honor

Like hard dry pomegranate skin

The wind goes so still

In Crete no one will take you up:

Offered small jade glass cups

Turn acrid water across the tongue.

2.

Some women dream rabbit, three in shadow,

Three in light

And there are others who, only a wolf inside the door

Few dream what hates:

Hard to confuse many by one

For the woman, call her Carrie

Who stays constant, leaves no one

Behind the door, silken among roses

Yes to her lover and yes again

No to abandonment, no

To the rabbit's fondling fur

In a dark lightly

The silhouette

She who arrives

3.

One woman says a soldier with a goat

Another says a soldier with a fox

And I say it is rarely the one you are with

But how you hold new love in your arms:

It is difficult not to be confused

I have been defeated by many

Less beautiful (Sylvia)

Who found me not

Nor would she sail to Crete

For me nor our other lovers

Nor did she offer clear wine or Iris—

Out on her own

The dark

Her shadow faint:

I must forget everyone

Why she would not rather see my wanting face

The cut light across the peach in my hand:

Rather the fat soldier exiled from Ithaca

Routed and scarred purple by Odysseus

      ] may that she not return]

      ] part my arms

      ] outward

      ] expectant

4

Mortal Esther—the sprung heart

Mother of Sylvia—stores lubricants I resist

To break open, soft pleasure:

O daughter, your mind

Is fading away, as never before. Resist my heart so close

Be deaf to your mother's

Long, dark shed

Enveloping your wings. Rough cats turn one

Slow frigates circle the granite mountain

The sun glints off their shingle-feathered wings

Still and extended:

Not one alights. But one, you who betray

Cow me with your scarred, frozen lips

Say nothing (as before, always) as to happiness or

Why you still will say nothing

Or what it is that you must resist

Across your heart? You never, now, will give in

To take me forward as once before. Why

Or for who, do you make wrong to Sappho?

For if you come, I will give in

For if you don't, I will give in further

To break once more free. I will be

Your enemy.

5.

]to reject

]not yet ripe

]neither virtuous nor complete

]though she pleases

]

]no other]thoughtless]silly

]

]

]heartless]tentative]I will not]not for you

]darkness

]

]the footfall

]

]pure crimson]

6.

Lucas, Pearl, my children

fraught with hurt. Reject aimless violence

Anything that pierces

Turn it away.

Eleanor, that love Diana performed, keep it

Make it a balm upon your enemies

Let it wrap their genitals in lavender

Multiply and lavish sweet pleasure

Harness what is dishonorable.

Make it a joy to throw it down.

Brother, sister

Grieve not the past

Pinch sweet lemon balm

Into the tea pot

Cup what is good

Keep what is evil

Dispense it to the winds

Now gone south.

7.

]

not

]

stop invisible [

]

does not

her bare throat [

]

not gold

]

Not.

8.

]Diana is afraid

]to make the command

]pride broken

]an elder now

]without mercy

]

[

9.

]

]

]not you, Regina

]

10.
]]

11.
]]]
]thoughtless
]her sandals
double-knotted.

12.

]damned

]

]

the things she offered

]

]bad luck on the mountain[

13.

Elizabeth, may you find her sweet

And be modest—do not mention me

How she would not come back

Whether or not I am bitter.

14.

At odds with me as ever,

Diana, you and your odd wardrobe

To which no one cottons

Never mind the rich without taste

I throw over all my awards

first at Art and then at Peace.

"Get out of Dodge" before you tamper

the crossings on the Road

Or, might I add, before you call

On your father and that sister, Eleanor

He with the bruised looking teats

And she with the two lost children

Unholy, ugly

Still not a maiden to touch

Sorry, but mind you, still pigeon-toed

Exit

Or, better yet

Don't even arrive.

15.

Maggie asleep (the wet, peach lip)

Does not

Quiet a story.

16.

]

]misfortune

]

]bad judgment

]misread North Star

]an emptiness

]

]soldiers at sea

]stillborn

]adrift

]

]

]harbor

]empty containers

]jolted

]

]no ease

]broken water[

]

]

17.

]

]

]charitable

]flush

]

]fresh skin, youth

[open] quick

]

]

]repellent] without song] flowerless

]

]sleep

]without a face]

]

18.

]

If yes, spring

]

19.

She refuses song

no *x* or *y*, musicians three

throw down their strings

(not once)

rejection haunts her tongue

No ripple in her dress

nor chatter from her anklets. She suffers

because he insists:

his body a stiff marble column

] Without a word

she refuses.

20.

]of lust lost

]

]once a swollen eye]

Regina.

21.

]the auburn in Eleanor I will not compare[

]the singular, immortal ones also reject

]not one iota in remorse

]may you go quick and distant

]a dry, cracked lake bed

]Libya

22.

In old age]

she forgets

some things]

]terrible]

]gone

]leave it at that.

23.

]

]silent harmonies]

]without shift

[no]

[no risk]

]

]

]the rising, full arch]

]

]

]joined

]

24.

]No, old man don't speak

]don't terrify us

]the proximity [death].

Each fears a funeral. Do you

know this? Please, delay the calling.

Tell the reaper to bury the iron tool.

]may we have new gods men, women, children

fresh on the porch, above the step.

25.

Noon]

Guys

Morning to night

Refuse to take a look

Even with the lupine bushes in our hair

And the occasional slap you give me on the butt

We should take to a room and fall asleep

Or wrap our arms around old men drunk

Already fast asleep on the City's benches.

]

If there is a bird in anybody's pants

It's lost its beak.

26.

She is neither equal nor a god.

She is perhaps most like you:

Mute, overlooking the cliff

There's no sugar on her tongue

A rasp for a whisper

Shakes nothing loose in my heart

I look away, desperate

Where is someone I can speak to?

Yes, the one with the pomegranate jewel

Bright red in her dark hair:

I am no longer blinded

There are honey hives in my ear

A chill separates from my skin

Released, marble turns liquid

Copper and white.

If I look closely there is a bleeding

What cuts close to the bone

A swallow—kind—in the breathing.

27.

]

]

Why not you, Eleanor?

Fresh oysters, ready to shuck!

28.

Stars with no moon luminous to a fault

here comes Mars

pink, full

and, oh, so close.

It's either Eleanor, Stephanie, Catherine or

here comes Isabelle.

]

29.

]

Chill me

Her fingers

Thin white lacework

Filigree on my shoulders

[

30.

]

]

Andrew

The joker dropped

Melissa a dead letter:

]

Out of Delphi—without a prayer

Indelicate Jane confuses seaweed with rope.

Burnt. Copper anklets and starched jeans.

Soon, after her mother caved in.

No one hears anything, travel a naysayer.

The daughters of Athena released the horses

Studs each gripped by the legs of Epidaurus' finest

The young men with taut ribbed torsos

]unlike to us

]not particular to the gods

To arrive in Attica

What is bitter in the tambourine and snare

Ill-fitted to the false speech of outsiders

]

A chorus in which no one transforms the anguish: Such sad, mean sounds

The streets filled with broken bricks

Folded down, broken statuary

Bitterroot and dry compost

The young on their horses in tears

The women in shredded pink silk

No one can call on anyone, absolutely

No one. The instruments fail. Every eye

And chin dropped: an ode for infinite loss,

Infinite forgiveness.

31.

As it is, shaggy Eric is fatherless

No son or golden-haired lover bears his name. Athena would not hand him a book

Or work as his messenger]

]cocksure, nobody has a clue

]not even the wanton are willing to come near

It is time for him to speak up, get another God to work his favors. A tame virgin with little

resistance, an unknown name]Pull down his pants. Pull his trigger.]Diana—sweet God with

the tiny hands—will surely reach out to lather his way.

Short and make it quick!

And she on a rough stone will not spread one leg or the other

]

32.

Hate crippled

heart twisted: cane without a path]

]

]

She refused to come and burnt my heart:

Distance quenches nothing, not even the ocean]

]

I hate you Eleanor, today, tomorrow, forever]

]You were such a fox on my doorstep

Even if she is not pretty to the eye

At least she is not evil as one knows who

Vanquished by hindsight.

33.

Shameless, I embrace the tree

Thick woven, fuzzy, red bark.

Thorns in the palms, graceless, I have turned her away.

]

Up from hell she arrives with a tiny black purse]

]

]

Wisteria breathes

Against my face

You will come my way

One breath at a time.]

34.

What city boy knocks you on your ass

His buckle halfway down to his knees?

35.

Tender my lips:

The guttural muffled trumpet

The fresh skin around my breasts

Unbearably dark hair

Goat thighs

Elk vagina

I did everything;

Impossible as Acacia & allergies

Bleeding the noses around us:

What is released

Goes to a deeper

What falls in a wild Iris

As much as I love the rough butch

Shadows and shade do not repel me.

36.

]

]new losses

bitter

Disabused, totally,

Nevertheless

A cancelled issue

Warps a wanted pattern:

Call me once more

Don't turn it into a battle

Cradle shadows on a red wall
Take me.

37.

Rope the Oak tree
Brave one
Gather bitter lemons
And then some
And for you
Lie down
On an alabaster pillow
Little devil. Take my Pleasure
blended as a pearl.
I will give you
Into a bed of small gods
Tiny features in their faces
Dimples and seizure.

38.

White dream

You come in a stream

Asleep, little devil, no pain

You would adhere lightning to water

The blessings shower and curl my hair,

Your hair and the hair of God's witness

You are no toy, nor am I:

Hear the oars paddling.

39.

Pussy?

Forget it absolutely

No cats

A goat,

well, the goat!

40.

To Stephanie

Over there, a limited estate

And no companions.

And, what can I say,

Prowling the coastline

A harpoon without pity

She rides a horse

With silk on the saddle.

41.

She swears against love

Not even the simplest reason:

I am set on the destruction

Of my own sweat and invention.

42.

I would not have killed

Then or now:

The irrational

Is no excuse for sacrifice.

Since I am still home

Convex by concave

The mirror within innocence

Ignored and rough tender:

Narcissus still virgin

Is awfully—note him there

By the still pool—

Awfully cranky.

Bend over,

Sweetly

43.

Stay home

The Marine Harmonica

Only plays for new wars

A guttural comb pinched with spit

The community is down to one solo.

]not you, Stephanie]no permission from here

]you hate displeasure]love burns]antiphonal

]mint bitter yodel]cuts the

44.

Eleanor

Stay the fuck

Away from Attica:

Bloated gutters, scratch

Filled songs, blistered voices,

No women, the absence of wind,

The death of rain, whiplash

In the front seat, the demolition derby

Wet circuits

Dry exits

Stay away.

45.

Sylvia! Permit me to turn

Calm my rage

Comb my heart:

A rack of small gold bells

The low hanging fuchsia

The red petals trembling, rain.

46.

Not everyone

Her feet

The ripple

In her toes.

Love her?

Yes, but slowly.

Let the lavender lilies fall from your hair

Cut and slice the fennel bulb into small

oiled pieces:

Let me tell you, blind I follow

each of your traces. Beauty in darkness charms.

Diana is more crumpled looking than Georgia.

47.

"Something else" Genuinely smart

Close to the heart

Her shape hardly matters.

Over there

It was yesterday

And for nothing.

Rough her up, Elizabeth

She can—to a degree—well, take it.

A young, very young, chick.

48.

]loud

]with your little axe

]Charles

]open my heart

]finger each and every louver]stop at nothing

]strip the sky

]velvet

Hot bust

The dip, the little arcs

Some say

A man.

49.

]calm]navel]

]

50.

In back

Take it off

Carefully

I will resist

Otherwise.

51.

Alli, you are so good willed,

I am afraid to touch you.

Not jeans: shorts stitched

White silicon

Hot gold zipper

Calves swollen

Shoestrings

Untied, dangling.

The varnished mirror

Pine—"tongue & groove"—floor.

Transparent blouse

Stripes of pink and magenta

What wraps your waist

White silk,

Floated gossamer.

52.

Boys, girls

What's the difference?

]

53.

She has No boys.

54.

...hat

the thin blue band]

over there green sky

smoking underskirt

the initial X

black no blue

a diamond

in the navel, silver sparks.

55.

She wants me, laughing;

Not a tear in her eye:

"Sappho, I am more than grateful, charmed, let me hold your ocelot."

Relax, sit down,

forget that I owe you and regret your timing.

I have to refuse

your intelligence and neglect

the warmth of your body.

There are no laurels for your hair, nor garnets

for your necklace

Nor slender squares of gold

To lace around your ankles

Nor polished abalone shells for your wrists:

Only a bitter oil

Cheap

To soothe your suffering:

I have no time to take you to bed

the harsh tarpaulin sheets

will abbreviate desire:

There is nothing sacred, no

place between my legs nor yours:

56.

Josephine

Rarely gives a thought

Turns on her sister

Sucks joy from the house

Is noted for courting the sky

When there is no moon

And the dancers remain

Vague shadows before the stars.

Dark she retreats around small ponds

Empty creeks and dead wells:

Field mice barely scuttle

And the dry grasses shrink

Yet, she rises slowly, a ghost

Without an iota of memory

What she hears, she swallows, forgets:

To avoid her

At all costs

Becomes conviction

I do it now with some ease

Rejection is not my normal lot

Sour plum juice

Nestled on my tongue:

On occasion one must spit

Their way to freedom

Before falling into the arms of new gods.

57.

Against my father

In his folded age

His hands tarred purple

His fingers and body so thin

The waves in his silver hair

An emblem to his son

A horse once rode there:

The starboard tack to the north

The rippled white sail spangled

Off the near coast

The City darkens.

58.

Not for you

I have absolutely nothing to offer

Your eyes drift aimless

The lover absolutely gone

An exile in your own body

Terrible as it is

I salute your absence;

A belt

The brass buckle

Fresh and newly shiny

I sent by a friend

To you in the north.

Father, I am no longer good with the sails:

The wind pushes south and my true love

]

59.

No, don't tell the groom

I will be angry in my own quiet

There is no statuary—no matter

The fluted dresses, the combed marble—The music is full of scratches

Nothing trembles

What might be gold, blackened silver.

In the grove

The groom in tears

Once for you.

Such large rain drops

So few Fingers

60.

Morning.

61.

She opens

The spray of gold ascendant pigeons

Mourning doves, too.

Drop gown,

Drop hand to knee.

No stars, black, your skin.

As white as the flesh on a skinned pear

Sliced in half, tilted on the dark saucer:

There is not a bent finger not ready to reach.

A [ ] singer with a terrible voice:

The white [   ] canvas tambourine.

62.

An unforgivable, bad drummer. No one takes out their sticks.

63.

Do I refuse to acknowledge my age?

Why does she tempt me like a young, startled, virgin?

]

Misshapen, fallen, muddied: An older, yet so tender swan.

]

Go where you can receive.

Her muse has such small hands.

Pointed egret feather gloves

Hunters abound looking for them.

64.

Take up the floor, Jack:

Rip it board by board.

If you are not enough, get a gang: Sylvia is approaching

Nothing equals what she's cost

Let her—her tight waist turning—Let her fall down

Let her fall way down.

65.

Heah, Geronicus, a divorce, just as you wanted;

A contract with no deal breaker

And you got the space she wanted

No longer buckled over, straight up on your legs:

66.

For every other girl on the block

And never again for you

Mr. Bridegroom

Never again for you.

67.

Old age:

Why are you running toward me?

I have not come for you

I have not come for you.

68.

The ex-housewife in sharp pink

Eliminates any comparison

To flat milk on a thin saucer:

The cat with a pink tipped tongue

Sipping too quickly

I now compare thee.

69.

Hello new bride

Hello groom

Make yourself at home:

I will go and corner the silk sheets.

70.

Welcome back, lover,

Welcome. And you? You, too.

71.

I am not some old shellfish—

You, Sylvia, can still bang me to pieces.

72.

Wet silk—hot tomato red—slipping.

73.

She is not someone who likes to love

But prefers the melancholy of a thin knife.

For some reason, she likes to hurt:

The silence in her elbows.

If you do not like me

Find another bed

Your youth is absolutely expendable.

74.

Pruning the roses: your already gnarled hand.

75.

]

She parallels the roses.

Please don't offer an unwashed hand.

Over there

The fake singers

Stomping the roses.

Not again

Jerks

76.

Sylvia, you love me by *the hatful*:

I worship your presence in the high mountains

The cut of spring water through round rock.

Eleanor has an ugly dog the color of mustard grass

Her nose constantly wet against Sylvia:

Even if it takes a small island far from Crete

She will be banished.

77.

I woke up out of a deep dream.

I could not recover you anywhere,

Elena.

78.

When did his son pander to Oedipus? The chill on his silver belt buckle.

The flattened cut cheekbone

Forebodes a dark winter:

Crow voice cut your volume,

The bellow in your wings.

You want me to say something honest

Maybe I will:

Attracted to what is defiled

Even though you yearn for beauty and virtue

Honesty will empower the play in your feet

Eyes will open the tongue into pure speech.

Sit down and look the opposite way.

Close your eyes. Imagine Sappho with wings.

79.

Witness Cynthia & just born Artemis:

You know what to do

Stroke the maidens

Unfold your garments

Two by two.

The bachelor suffered terribly

Before courtship the wine glass

Singular, half-full and transparent:

She held an empty glass by the stem

Walked in circles by the oak

The wilted purple vines in the near field:

Good things do not always happen

To couples.

80.

]

Brandy heirloom tomatoes, the juices]

81.

]

Cynthia & Cato were robbed by friendship.

Not enough, never, N's cupidity so senseless.

She's one of those who can't get enough.

Listen to the pain in their lament.

82.

To change the river, toss a pebble.

Let me have at her, and the nectarine, too.

No one will read this ever, well, not ever.

So much of you & I will be forgotten. Bet on it.

Broke and sanctimonious is rarely good.

Yet wealth and virtue—is it always interesting?

83.

All day long, amazing, this erection!

During the afternoon

It's sometimes more quick

Yet—whatever it is—elevates us.

]it is always extraordinary

that ecstasy should overtake and please us.

Right in the throat, night or day, this white ball, luminous, spinning:

Under morning foot. The rising arch:

White, a bead of sperm, separated.

84.

Illuminated, then not, the quality of despair.

When the sun rose—all rays—We walked into it, ablaze.

-

85.

A short, sustained hello to Julia, bubbling, Gloria's child.

Get going. Your age and wrinkles offer me nothing.

86.

]

Not as compelling as a harmonica in a riff, silver, rather than gold.

]

You broke the strings on my guitar]

thin brass shavings, everywhere.

]Bad boy dusk

To take in your svelte tongue: fluttering.

87.

With love animated, under the heart, swelling sorrow.

Not I, not hate, no companions, please.

Not I, nor your henchmen, Elizabeth

Forget her, guys,

Let her fold her clothes to dry

in a perfectly small City.

]

88.

]

With no hands]

89.

]

Between whose hands?

90.

Your ex?

91.

Singularly, he rejects each son.

92.

Which woman is not?

93.

Catherine says Theona threw out the jet black, ruby ring

Once given to her by her late father.

A black glint on a thin silver, crescent blade.

Transparent amber olive oil in a porcelain dish:

a thin black streak, coiled.

94.

Mars gone

and the gray cloud cover

Early morning, no sun, together, over the pillow.

]

]neighborhood

]a brown patch in the bougainvillea.]

Fallen, unable to part

Funeral leftovers.

95.

Leda, certainly.

]

Divorce: alimony, booty.

96.

Eleanor

97.

Ecstasy planter

A root that rips up sidewalks

Block-a-dock

Crepuscule gossamer, underwear:

98.

Cancelled

99.

Refuses to come out:

Wing spread, the ascent

Safe passage

Stephanie, again

Tanya, ah, Tanya

100.

Myth breaker

Ambrosia

No skill, an absolute natural:

101.

Onyx, her breast cups.

Stephen Vincent is a bookman. Poet, editor, publisher, and all-around bibliophile, he has during the past few years turned to making a form of writing he calls haptic drawing. His most recent poetry books include *After Language: Letters to Jack Spicer* (BlazeVox, 2012), *Walking* (Junction Press, 1996), and *Walking Theory* (Junction Press, 2006), and the e-book *Triggers* (Shearsman, 2004). From 1972 to 1981, he was the publisher of Momo's Press, which first introduced the work of such poets and writers as Ntozake Shange, Victor Hernandez Cruz, Hilton Obenzinger, Beverly Dahlen, and Jessica Hagedorn. In the eighties, he was the director of Bedford Arts, Publishers, which became internationally recognized for the publication of books featuring the works of Masahisa Fukase, David Park, Roy DeForest, Miriam Schapiro, Mark Klett, and Christo. Throughout his career, Vincent has occasionally taught creative writing at schools that have included the University of Nigeria, San Francisco State University, and the San Francisco Art Institute. Since 2007, in addition to writing, his drawings have been featured in gallery shows at Braunstein/Quay (San Francisco), 2009; Steven Wolf Fine Arts (San Francisco), 2009; Jack Hanley Gallery (New York), 2011; and Anglim/Trimble (San Francisco). The haptics are an implicit part of three of his books: *The First 100 Days of Obama* (Steven Wolf Fine Arts, 2009), *The Last 100 Days of the Presidency of Barack Obama* (Book Studio, 2017), and *Haptics: The Novel* (XEXOXIAL Editions, 2013). Stephen Vincent resides in San Francisco.

Made in the USA
Las Vegas, NV
26 December 2023

83485114R00042